Dutch Ov(

The Best Food You Will Ever Eat

Cooked Over a Campfire

Dr. Michael Stachiw and Michael Stachiw, Jr.

August 2012

ISBN-13: 978-1479133284

ISBN-10: 1479133280

Special thanks to Kevin Cusack and Lauren Gatcombe for their input

Dutch Oven Cooking

The Best Food You Will Ever Eat Cooked Over a Campfire

By

Dr. Michael Stachiw and Michael Stachiw, Jr.

Table of Contents

The Challenge

It sounds almost like a line from the TV series "Survivor", but a challenge it is. If you think about it too much, you might even scare yourself off from the task. To prepare meals over an open fire, where you have little control over the temperature, the duration/quality of the fire and the overall weather conditions. Less than an ideal situation to begin any venture, but one that each outdoor chef faces and must master.

It takes all kinds to make a successful campout. Camping should be a relaxing activity that connects us with nature, but often it turns into Cowboys v. Indians meets Lord of the Flies. The mesh of different personalities in an unfamiliar environment causes much strife. Dutch Oven cooking, when done right, calms the mind and nourishes the body. When everyone is eating some of the best food they have ever eaten ("Hunger is the best condiment" - as the Ancient Greeks would say) around a campfire or sitting on a picnic bench, people come together.

Michael and Dr. Mike have prepared meals both for themselves as well as groups of others in all sorts of situations. The least favorable would be in the pouring rain with a steady howling wind, to the most favorable of being a semi-cool day, with not a cloud insight and perfect coals around our Dutch ovens. However, the majority of our meals have been prepared in situations between these two extreme situations. But, (don't you just love that word, because you know what's going to be said next) you should always be prepared for the worst case situation, and hopefully realize a best case set of circumstances.

One thing that is very important for the reader of this book is to realize that Dr. Mike and Michael are heavy in to Boy Scouts, outdoor recreation, overnight camping and yes simply sleeping out amongst the stars. In addition, both dedicate a large portion of their free time to outdoor youth causes and group camping events. You might question why this is important information? The answer is that unlike a majority of outdoor cooks, both Michael and Dr. Mike are regularly called upon to cook for large groups of individuals on an outdoor setting, leading to both time-tested as well as crowd-tested recipes and cooking techniques.

Dr. Mike would pass along the following piece of information: "when cooking outdoors the old adage of planning your work and then working your plan can not be under emphasized. And to which the Murphy's Law should always be respected, that is what can go wrong, will go wrong, and will go wrong at the worst possible moment."

Camping doesn't have to be miserable. When we cook food in a Dutch Oven, most people come up to us in amazement asking how we can do it or saying they had no idea you could do that. There is much more to outdoor cookery than hotdogs on an open fire or grey mystery meat being cooked on a decade-old outdoor grill.

Luxury suite in the high Colorado mountains… the chef plans his gift to humanity: Dutch Oven food.

The Fire

Without fire, little cooking would occur. Unlike indoor cooking where you have microwave, gas and electric stoves/ovens, in the outdoor arena you only have fire. There are three sources of fire used in outdoor cooking, and usually an outdoor chef will use all three when preparing a meal. These sources are:

Wood fire – This is a general purpose fire, most useful for warming up the cook and all the campers. At the end of the day, the camp wood fire becomes the focus of fellowship. This type of fire is also referred to as a friendship fire.

Charcoal fire - A cooking fire and the source of coals for Dutch ovens. Usually this fire will be hotter and more focused than the wood fire. Two advantages a charcoal fire has over a wood fire is the constant temperature over a longer period of time and less off flavors introduced into the food being cooked.

To start a charcoal fire you will need the following items:

- o Newspaper
- o Strike Anywhere matches
- o Charcoal chimney
- o Charcoal (I almost always have two 20 pound bags on hand)

To light the charcoal, place a loosely wadded piece of regular newspaper (not the glossy Sunday advertising type of paper) in the bottom of the charcoal chimney. We usually will place a few small sticks on top of the newspaper and then place charcoal on top of the newspaper. Using the strike anywhere matches light the newspaper from the bottom of the chimney (lift it up!) and wait. You should have hot coals in about 15 to 20 minutes time.

Gas fire – A cooking fire, used for frying and boiling. If you have a reflection oven (i.e. camp oven) this is also a good source of fire for baking.

Friendship Fire – a fire to sit around, talk, and even eat by, but almost never is used for cooking anything other than marshmallows on a skewer. This type of fire is constructed using local wood, of varying thickness and dryness. Two of the main reasons a friendship fire is never used for cooking are: 1) off flavors get into your food from the wood, and 2) it is nearly impossible to control the temperature with any degree of accuracy.

Fire Safety – regardless of the type of fire you will be using, please remember that you are in the outdoors and need to take precautions against letting the fire get away from you. Minimally you need to have on hand two buckets of water in the vicinity of each fire you make.

Before starting your fire, be sure to clear the area of flammable material not directly being used in the construction of the fire. Not all things that might start out as being a fire hazard can become one, but for example grass that is green will dry out quickly next to a fire and allow it to grow outside your intended area.

Entire dinner meal for 25 people

The Tools

A samurai is not much without his sword. The chef is nothing with his tools. When cooking, you will at a minimum need 2 (preferably cast iron) skillets, 2 Dutch Ovens, and a stainless steel pot. You can do a lot with just those items. Obviously included in the must-haves are gloves, spices, a stove, charcoal, and matches, but the focus of this chapter is "where the magic happens".

Cast iron skillets are tough. They are heavy. They get the job done. They give your food more flavor. They last longer. Some argue they are easier to clean. Cooking is much simpler using a big honking skillet in the outdoors. If you are backpacking in the Appalachians, then you surely would want to use a normal kitchen skillet because of the superior weight. This chapter (book actually) is going with the assumption that your car is <5 mins. away so weight is not that determinative of a factor.

Dutch Ovens are God's gift to the outdoors. They act just like an oven in a normal kitchen. Just use more coals instead of turning the dial to the right temperature. You want pizza? You want quiche? You want BBQ pork loin? You want a turkey? All that and more can be done in a Dutch Oven. There are literally thousands of recipes out there on the internet. Just search for "Dutch Oven recipes". The reason you want a minimum of 2 Dutch Ovens is so you can make (at least) 1 main course that can feed many or a main course and either a side or dessert that can feed a more modest amount. Dutch Ovens take time. Don't be surprised if that turkey you need to cook for 6 takes 2.5-3.25 hours to cook in a Dutch Oven. It takes time, but the satisfaction of "real food" is worth it.

One last item that was added later in our campout kitchen is a Camp Oven that goes on a stovetop. It is not required but highly recommended. We make cookies every campout in the afternoon now because the camp oven is so incredibly easy to use.

Cast Iron Skillet

Stainless steel pot

Scouts go wild over fresh cookies

Basic Food Handling

Dr. Mike washing his hands before acquiring food from the quartermaster for mid-day meals

It's often said that "cleanliness is next to godliness"[1], but in food preparation and handling you cannot have too much cleanliness. It should also go without saying; the proper handling of food is the most important aspect of cooking, even more important that all the recipes in the world combined! No matter how good the food tastes, if the crew you are feeding get sick from food poisoning, that's all that will be remembered about that meal, and it can even result in serious harm to those eating the food.

There are five basic areas of food handling that need to be addressed:

- Cleanliness – keeping all aspects of the kitchen clean

- Separating Foods – cross contamination between food sources

[1]Full quotation is: 'Cleanliness is next to Godliness.' The latter quality, as displayed in a Russian devotee, is more allied with dirt than anything else.
[1876 F. G. Burnaby *Ride to Khiva* x.]

- Cooking – the actual cooking process

- Chilling – keeping ingredients and finished products cool

- Animal Control – you are outdoors and animals want your food also

Cleanliness:

Cleanliness starts with washing hands. Be sure to always use soap and warm (the hotter the better) water when washing your hands. You should also make it a habit to wash your hands often during food preparation, cooking and serving. For example, after handling meat, fish or poultry, you would want to wash your hands, so that later when you might be handling cheese or bread (items that might not be cooked during the meal being prepared) so that any germs on the raw meat was not carries over to the bread or cheese.

You should always wash with hot water before use any utensils, cutting boards, knives, dishes and table/counter tops. Even if it was cleaned yesterday, you might have had insect or other visitors who touched your tools during the night. Remember you are preparing food in an outdoor environment, which you have less control over when compared to indoor kitchens. Dust, pollen and other airborne pollutants/contaminants are also a factor when cooking outdoor, so again washing tools right before use is a sage suggestion.

It should also be stressed that all utensils, cutting boards, dishes, knives etc should be cleaned after use, and as a general rule they should be cleaned again (preferably I a dish washer) when you get home.

There are also some tips/tricks when cooking outdoors that may sound counter-intuitive, but will greatly reduce cleanup and increase the overall cleanliness of your outdoor kitchen. These include:

- Use paper towels for most of your food preparation cleanup. Unless you have a large supply of clean cloth towels on hand, you would not want to use a cloth towel to clean up blood or fish juices and then later use the same towel to dry your hands.

- Use disposable eating utensils, plates, and cups. Kitchen and dining cleanup is probably one o f the worst/hardest areas to do properly in the outdoor kitchen environment. Without having running hot water, garbage disposal and other modern kitchen cleanup facilities, usage of the disposable items just makes sense.

- Always have on hand a large pump dispenser of hand sanitizer. This is not a substitute for washing your hands, but it is also a way to ensure that your guests will have relatively germ free hands for eating.

- You should also have a supply of sanitizing wipe (baby style wipes) to use for intermediate wiping down of tables and other surfaces that might come in contact with food.

- Use only plastic cutting boards. It is almost impossible, even under the best circumstances, to get a wood cutting board entirely germ free.

Separate:

Keeping foods before and after they are cooked separated reduces the changes of cross –contamination from occurring and usually greatly reduces the overall hassled of storing and transporting food ingredients. This is best explained through this scenario: You have bread, cheese, raw poultry, milk and potatoes. You would want to keep the cheese, raw poultry and milk chilled the bread and potatoes dry. However you would also want to keep the milk and cheese in a separate cooler than the raw poultry. Why? If you think about a package of poultry, it often leaks (leaking raw chick juices) that you would not want to have come in contact with the cheese (which might be eaten raw) nor the container of milk (juices might get on the lips of the milk jug). I would also think that keeping bread dry would be self explanatory.

To further this concept of separation and cross-contamination you should follow these tips:

- Use different cutting boards for each raw and cooked food item. Never (never!) use a cutting board that was used to cut up raw food ingredients to cut up cooked food items.

- Always wash hands, cutting boards, and utensils with hot soapy water after each food ingredient has been chopped/cut up.

- Never use a bowl, plate or other contained to hold cooked food that had been used earlier with raw food ingredients.

Cooking:

Before starting to cook (heat the raw materials) review the desired end temperature/state of the food items. For example if you are cooking a pork loin, double check that you will want to reach a temperature of at least 140F and that you have a meat thermometer to check the temperature. Cooking food ingredients for the correct length of time, at the correct temperature, and reaching the desired end temperature are the surest way to ensure that all harmful bacteria will be killed during the process. One simple way to remember the rules of safe cooking is the jingle "bacteria multiply between 40F and 140F".

The following coking guidelines provided by the USDA and Partnership for Food Safety Education:

- Always use a clean thermometer to verify that meat, poultry, casseroles and other food is completely cooked all the way through. It is best to use a meat thermometer for this task

- Cook roasts and steaks to at least 145F.

- Poultry should be cooked to 180F

- Ground beef should be cooked to at least 160F

- Cook eggs until the yolk and white are firm. Never use partially cook or raw eggs (unless the final food item is to be cooked to at least 140F, like a cake)

- Fish should be opaque and flake easily with a fork

- Safe Cooking Temperatures - As measured with a food thermometer. (from Partnership for Food Safety Education website http://www.fightbac.org/safe-food-handling/cook/127-cook-heat-it-up-chart)

Ground Meat & Meat Mixtures	
Beef, Pork, Veal, Lamb	160 °F
Turkey, Chicken	165 °F
Fresh Cuts Pork, Beef, Veal, Lamb	
Plus 3 minutes stand time for safety	145 °F
Poultry	
Chicken & Turkey, whole	165 °F
Poultry Parts	165 °F
Duck & Goose	165 °F
Stuffing (cooked alone or in bird)	165 °F
Ham, Cooked and Fresh	
Ham (raw) Plus 3 min. stand	145 °F

time	
Pre-cooked (to reheat)	140 °F
Eggs & Egg Dishes	
Eggs	Cook until yolk & white are firm
Egg Dishes	160 °F
Seafood	
Fin fish	145 °F or until opaque & flakes easily with fork
Shrimp, Lobster & Crabs	Flesh pearly & opaque
Clams, Oysters & Mussels	Shells open during cooking
Scallops	Milky white or opaque & firm
Casseroles	165 °F

Chilling:

Most of the sage advice on chilling of foods usually deals with leftovers. However in the outdoor kitchen, there is usually very little leftovers, or there is no provision for the safe storage of leftovers. However, a more important issue for the outdoor kitchen is the keeping of frozen and refrigerated food ingredients. When preparing for an outdoor cooking

19

event, always take at least one extra cooler for the storage of ice and nothing else. Also it is usually easier to use "blue ice" instead of ice for most of the coolers as there is no ice melt to deal with, which has ruined more than one raw ingredient needed for a meal. But with that said, "real" ice does keep frozen foods more frozen than blue ice. So, to compensate we suggest the following:

- Use real ice for the storage of frozen foods. For example frozen turkey breasts or frozen juice.

- Use blue ice for items that will not be stored frozen, like milk, eggs, milk etc.

- Foods that will be used on day two or three of a campout, and that can be frozen should be frozen.

- Don't open the spare ice storage container, unless you need the ice in one of the other ice chests

- Drain daily any ice melt that occurs in the real ice/frozen ice chests

Animal Control:

One area of food safety that gets forgotten all too often is the wildlife that inhabits the same forest that you are camping in. Animals such as ants, squirrels, chipmunks and raccoons (let alone bears, which is a whole different topic for discussion) will run through your outdoor kitchen area at night. Both from a food safety viewpoint, as well as not loosing you food, you need to protect your food from these animals. Tips for safe keeping of you the food include:

- Keep food as long as possible in your car before use

- Food ingredients like sugar, flour, cake mix, etc. should be kept in a water-tight container like a screw top 5 gallon pail.

- If ice chests are to be left outside overnight, put heavy items like bags of charcoal on top so the animals can not open the lid of the ice chest.

- During food preparation, fats, greases, and drippings should be disposed of as far away from the campsite as possible.

- After every meal, all disposable dishes, cans and leftover food should be bagged and toted to a disposal era (or dumpster).

- Always police and remove to all candy wrappers, napkins, etc that might have blown around.

Camp Kitchen Management

Dr. Mike cleaning a 12 inch iron frying pan

Without writing an entire handbook on the running of a camp kitchen, it should be recognized that three main areas exist in the successful preparation of food. 1) Purchasing of food ingredients, 2) people who are responsible for preparing the food, and 3) there is a definite timeline to the preparation of any meal.

Purchasing Food Ingredients:

Acquiring the necessary ingredients for your meals should not be a major task, but some planning on your part will go a long way on successful meal preparation. The first step after deciding on what foods to prepare for each of your meals will be the calculation of amount of required ingredients. Some foods are easy to calculate, for example ears of corn for corn on the cob. For adults 1 to 1.5 ears each should be enough, while half ears for the younger set should suffice. Meat is a little bit trickier. The general rule of thumb for meat is that you end up with between 3 to 4 oz of cooked meat per person. The trick part is that meat shrinks as it cooks, and different cuts of meat shrink at different rates.

Use the tables in the chapter "How much meat to buy" to estimate the correct sizes to buy.

If you are only cooking for 2 or 3 people then shopping at your normal grocery store for the food ingredients is the way to go. However, if you are cooking for a large group, then you might want to consider shopping at a discount warehouse store, not only because it is usually cheaper, but that the food items come in larger containers making the whole process simpler.

One often overlooked aspect of camp cooking, is that since we are in a limited kitchen, usually without a microwave, running water, etc. the use of pre-pared food items should not be overlooked. For example, I almost always used canned/jars of spaghetti sauce for my lasagnas, spaghetti and other pasta dished instead of trying to make this sauce in the camping environment. The same goes for the gray I use in my biscuits and gravy breakfast offering. The canned sausage gravy make the preparation of this meal a real delight and it can be time in a timely fashion.

The other aspect of food purchasing, is that you should always have a selection of standard ingredients/seasonings on hand that you take from campout t campout. In my kitchen I have a spice pail and a dry goods pail.

Your selection should include the following:

- Salt

- Pepper

- Baking Powder

- Flour

- Sugar

- Brown Sugar

- Oil (for cooking and for Dutch oven protection)

- Cinnamon

- Steak Seasoning Rub

- Poultry Seasoning Rub

- Other spices as desired

- Matches (to light the camp stove and charcoal)

People Management:

It is often said that a chef is like an emperor of their domain. This might sound pompous, but you cannot have people wandering in and out of a kitchen, sneaking snacks of partially cooked food and think that you will end up with the meal you thought you were going to make. So as a general rule, only those responsible for preparing the meal should be in the kitchen during cooking. It is also important that you identify the following roles and the people to fill then before getting started. You will need:

- Fireman (person who make the coals used by the Dutch ovens)

- Cook (person actually cooking the food)

- Support (people who peel potatoes, crack the eggs open, etc)

Note if the group is small, one person might fill all three roles, but in all of the large groups that we have cooked for, you usually need these three roles filled separately.

Typical Outdoor Kitchen Setup. Notice that the yellow box containing cooking supplies is under the roof

Cooking Timeline:

The more complicated topic is the time line to outdoor preparation of a meal. You will need lead time to prepare the food ingredients (i.e., peel potatoes, crack eggs and chop meat up); you will also need lead time to get the coals started, and then the actual cook time. In some cases you will also need some time after the food is prepared to get it ready to be served. The best way figure out your time line is to start backwards from the serving time. For example, let's say we are going to serve a meal at 6:00 PM and the longest cooking food items takes 3.5 hours, and we think it will take approximately 30 minutes to get the coals ready, and then we need to start the cooking process at 2:00 PM. However we will need to prepare the ingredients before the cooking process which usually takes between a half an hour to an hour… so your real start time for the meal is more like 1:00 PM… right after you have cleaned up from serving lunch!

A second complication to your time line is that not all foods take the same time to cook or prepare. For example turkey breasts might take 3 hours to cook, but the corn on the cob only takes 30 minutes. So you must prioritize your time to the longest cooking ingredient first then to the next longest and so on. Also do not forget, nor underestimate the preparation time required for some dishes. Preparing lasagna can take easily an hour to brown the meat, boil the noodles and layer the sausage/meat/cheese/noodles in the Dutch oven even before you begin the "cooking" process, while in contrast cooking of pork loins takes approximately 3 hours with only about 15 minutes of precooking preparation required.

White 5 gallon bucket for collecting grease

Dutch Ovens & Cast Iron Cookware

One of the biggest secrets to outdoor cooking is cast iron cookware. In today's 'hi-tech' world, it is all too easy to think that only lightweight aluminum or steel Teflon coated cookware along with gas fired stoves can a meal be prepared. However one of the required skills taught during Boy Scout adult leader training is using a Dutch oven. Almost all "newbie" scout leaders moan and groan in advance of this training because it sounds like something that harks back to the early days of scouting when travel to campouts was conducted on mule. The real surprise is just how versatile and useful a Dutch oven can be (and any Scout Leader who sticks with scouting for a period longer than a couple of years, have all fallen in love with their Dutch ovens).

The reason cast iron cookware works as well as it does, it does to the mass, or weight, of the cookware. As an example, if you were to place a piece of food in aluminum foil and place it into the fire, you probably would only have a minute or so before the food went from cooked to burnt, however the same piece of food place into a Dutch oven or fry pan could probably sit for 15 minutes before it would be cooked and another 15 minutes before it started to burn. This "delay" may sound like a drawback, but in reality when cooking outdoors, and if like us you are cooking for a large crowd, this delay actually turns into another method of controlling the heat, cook times and eventually providing a mechanism for bringing the entire meal together. Another advantage of cast iron is that just like it takes time to heat up it also takes longer to cool down, thus keeping food warmer longer.

Selecting Cast Iron Cookware

Like all of your camping equipment, a certain amount of understanding into the pros and cons of different cast iron cookware is required to get the most out of the equipment.   It should be noted, that when we refer to cast iron cookware, we are referring to "native" cast iron cookware and not cookware coated with enamel or any other covering as we have found this type of cookware does not fare well in the outdoor cooking environment. Also, there is a whole line of aluminum "cast iron style" cookware out there, but we have little experience with this line of equipment (but at some time in the future we both hope to gain experience).

Pro's to Cast Iron Cookware:

- o Heat retention
- o Heat resistance
- o Ease of cleaning

Con's of Cast Iron Cookware:

- o Weight. This stuff can be heavy
- o Amount of post cooking maintenance required
- o Pitting of the cooking surface over time
- o Reaction of food with the iron surface
- o Retention of flavors from meals past

With this list in mind, the following is a list of things to look for when buying your cast iron cookware:

o Do not get more pot or pan than you need for the occasion. Remember cast iron cookware is heavy without food in it. If you finish cooking and cannot lift the pot or pan, then you have a problem. Dutch oven sizes serve approximately (and what normally is served in that size Dutch Oven):

DUTCH OVEN SIZE	OVEN CAPACITY	TYPES OF DISHES	# PERSONS SERVED
8"	2 Quarts	Vegetables, Desserts	2-4
10"	4 Quarts	Beans, Rolls, & Cobblers	4-7
12"	6 Quarts	Main & Side Dishes, Rolls, Desserts	12-14
12" Deep	8 Quarts	Turkeys, Hens, Hams, Standing Rib Roasts	16-20
14"	8 Quarts	Main & Side Dishes, Rolls, Potatoes, Desserts	16-20
14" Deep	10 Quarts	Turkeys, Hens, Hams, Standing Rib Roasts	22-28
16"	12 Quarts	Large Group Events	22-28

o   Pans should have sturdy handles. The handles on Dutch ovens also need to be sturdy but also need to be easily moved aside for access to the lid.

o   Lids need to tightly fit on pots, otherwise moisture will escape during the cooking process

o   All handles and lids need to be made of cast iron or steel. Remember you will be placing hot coals against the top and bottom of these pots and pans

o   Dutch ovens should have three legs on them[2]

o   Dutch oven lids should have a lip of about one inch or so (keeps the coals from falling off when you take the lid off)

Seasoning Cast Iron Cookware[3]

Before you use your cast iron cookware for the first time, you need to "season" it. Some cast iron cookware, for example that sold by Lodge[4], comes pre-seasoned, but the majority of cast iron cookware comes from the factory with a light covering of wax or mineral oil that needs to be removed before you cook food in it and you need to place the initial protective layer of vegetable oil on the cast iron.

---

[2] If you are going to use your Dutch ovens on a gas stove, the three legs is not required
[3] Utah State University Extension bulletin
[4] Lodge Manufacturing Company

There are two basic methods to seasoning your cast iron cookware, and this is the one time that you will use a diluted solution of soapy water during the cleaning of cast iron.

Regular Oven Method: With soapy water, wash your oven and rinse thoroughly and dry. Oil all surfaces and pour about 1 tablespoon of oil in the Dutch oven, or other cast iron cookware. With a cotton cloth, rub all the surfaces. Add enough oil to cover the bottom of the Dutch oven. Place in 350 °F. Oven for 30 minutes. Remove from oven and carefully circulate the oil to cover all of the sides and bottom. Add more oil and heat in 200 °F. Oven for one hour. Turn the oven off and leave overnight. In the morning, rub all surfaces with remaining oil and remove excess oil. Now it's ready to use.

On the Fire Method: Wash with soapy water. Rise with clean water. Now fill partially again with clean water and bring to a boil. Drain hot water, and if needed dry thoroughly. Add vegetable oil to the bottom (inside cooking surface) of the cast iron cookware and then rub this oil all over the cookware.

Controlling the Heat

When outdoor cooks talk about temperature control, they are either referring to the temperature of the fire or the temperature of their Dutch ovens. In either case, they are referring to their attempt to control the cooking temperature. This is partially why no two meals cooked outdoors taste the same.

For general cooking, like frying or simmer food where an open fire, be it wood or charcoal, the following method works well:

Hold your palm at the place where food will go, over coals for broiling, in front of reflector oven for baking. Count "one-one-thousand, two-one-thousand" and so on for the number of seconds you can stand to hold your hand there. You should never hold your hand close to a fire in a manner to which you might get burned. The chart below translates loosely the number of seconds you could hold your hand near the fire to the relative cooking temperature provided.

Hand Holding Time	Heat	Temperature
6 to 8 seconds	Slow	250°F - 350°F
4 to 5 seconds	Moderate	350°F - 400°F
2 to 3 seconds	Hot	400°F - 450°F

Hand Holding Time	Heat	Temperature
1 or less seconds	Very Hot	450°F - 500°F

In contrast, controlling the temperature of a Dutch oven is more straightforward. For each charcoal briquette placed on top of the Dutch oven, or that the Dutch oven rests on, you can assume 20 to 30°F (I always assume 25°F per briquette) of cooking heat.

Another aspect of your Dutch Oven is that it provides a variety of cooking techniques that only differ by where the heat is applied.

Cooking Technique	Description

Cooking Technique	Description
ROASTING	The heat source should come from the top and bottom equally. Coals should be placed under the oven and on the lid at a 1 to 1 ratio.
BAKING	Usually done with more heat from the top than from the bottom. Coals should be placed under the oven and on the lid at a 1 to 3 ratio, having more on the lid.
FRYING, BOILING	All of the heat should come from the bottom. Coals will be placed under the oven only.
STEWING, SIMMERING	Almost all heat will be from the bottom. Place the coals under and on the oven at a 4 to 1 ratio with more underneath than on the lid.

Cleaning Cast Iron Cookware

One of the major advantages to cooking with cast iron cookware is the ease of cleanup. Some people even refer to cast iron cookware as the original "no stick" cookware. Even though this is an over simplification, the ease of cleanup is true.

For cast iron cookware, the cleaning process is in two steps.

1) Food is removed: To remove stuck on food, place some warm clean water into the oven and heat until almost boiling. Using a plastic mesh scrubber or coarse sponge and NO SOAP[5], gently break loose the food and wipe away.

---

[5] Soap is not recommended because its flavor will get into the pores of the metal and will taint the flavor of your next meal. The exception to the "no soap" rule is when you first purchase an un-seasoned piece of cast iron cookware.

After all traces have been removed, rinse with clean warm water and heat again to a boil. Pour the boiling water off and dry with a soft cloth or paper towel.

While the cast iron cookware is still hot, and after the moisture from the place a thin coating of vegetable oil[6] on the inside (cooking side) of your pots and Dutch ovens.

---

[6] Never use mineral or motor oil on your cast iron cookware.

Allow the cast iron cook ware to cool completely before placing into storage. If the cook ware is a Dutch oven, it is recommended that a folded paper towel be placed between the lid and the pot body to allow air to flow inside the Dutch oven.

Usually the outside of your cast iron cook ware will need very little maintenance, but a little vegetable oil rubbed on the outside will keep the rust away.

Handling Cast Iron Pots & Pans

Novices using cast iron cookware for the first time, can easily reach the conclusion that cast iron cookware is indestructible. I can see how somebody might think this given the heaviness and mass of the cookware, but an overlook facet of cast iron is the crystalline structure of the metal. If you place cast iron, while empty into a fire, or drop the cast iron on a hard surface like concrete it will break.

This is a picture of one of my favorite Dutch ovens that fell out of my truck during unloading after a campout, and as you can see it is now ruined. Cast iron cannot be repaired!

Here is a list of "No No's" for the handling of cast iron that we want to pass along to you.

1. Never allow cast iron to sit in water or allow water to stand in or on it. It will rust despite a good coating. If it is being used during the rainy part of the year, you need to turn fry pans and other open cast iron cookware upside down so that any rusting occurs on the outside of the cooking utensil if they get wet. As a rule of thumb, we do this every night just in case the weatherman doesn't know what he is talking about.

2. Never use soap on cast iron. The soap will get into the pores of the metal and won't come out very easy, but will return to taint your next meal. If soap is used accidentally, the oven should be put through the pre-treatment procedure, including removal of the present coating.

3. Do not place an empty cast iron pan or oven over a hot fire. Aluminum and many other metals can tolerate it better but cast iron will crack or warp, ruining it.

4. Do not get in a hurry to heat cast iron, you will end up with burnt food or a damaged Dutch oven or pan.

5. Never put cold liquid into a very hot cast iron pan or oven. They will crack on the spot.

How we transport our many Dutch Ovens. Be careful though

Early Morning Essentials

One of the drawbacks usually associated with outdoor/camp cooking is the lack of specialized pots and tools. For example, you might be lucky enough to actually have a camp coffee pot, but what do you do if half of your crew prefers hot coca instead? Or, you might also have a bunch of guests who drink coffee, but prefer the decaffeinated kind. Without having 6 burners on a stove, or a microwave, this could prove to be a problem. Well this is one of those situations where technology has come to the aid of the camp cook.

One of the first things we do in the morning is to bring a big "coffee pot" of water to a boil. This pot is used solely for the purpose of heating water for beverages and cooking purposes. We also stock in our supplies instant cocoa, coffee "tea bags" (both caffeinated and decaffeinated) and some tea bags. We also have a few of the instant creamers and sweeteners on hand for those that need it. By having fresh hot morning beverages, the people we are cooking for will wait (sometimes for extended periods of time) without grumbling for us to finish preparing the morning meal. We would also mention that this can be one of the pivotal turning points for "converting" somebody to how fun and comfortable camping can be.

Unless we know in advance what each person prefers for their hot beverage, we almost always bring enough of each beverage (coffee, tea and coca) for each for every day we are camping.

Standard Fare

Kevin Cusack, who helped greatly with this book, with his favorite Dutch oven glove

Standard fare is a collection of recipes or menus that we have compiled that are almost used in 95% of all campouts. This doesn't mean that we don't cook other things, but as an example have you ever been on a campout that didn't somehow utilize bacon, eggs and bread? I bet not!

We would also like to note that in our "standard fare" collection of recipes, we are presenting the basic skills required of any outdoor chief. If you cannot prepare these dishes, you need to consider doing something different on a campout.

Bacon, Fried

What camp breakfast is complete without the smell of bacon cooking in the early morning light? Preparation is easy as long as you do not try and rush the cooking. If you are going to be cooking eggs or French toast as part of your breakfast menu, do not wipe the pan after you drain the grease out.

Place bacon in pan and cook. Do not consume raw. You can add seasoning if you desire, but it is not required.

Suggested Fire:

- o   Gas camp stove fire

Tools Required:

- o Cast iron frying pan
- o Spatula

Ingredients:

- o Bacon

Service Size: 4 people per ½ lb of bacon

Preparation:

Just throw it in there

Cast iron improves the taste

Keep your spices handy

Baked Beans

Baked beans are a campout classic. Very easy to make. You put however many cans of beans in your Dutch Oven you want. You then can either put in sliced pieces of fried bacon and/or brown sugar. Both make it taste better. Cook beans until hot. Some people taste the iron in the beans (due to the fact that the bean juice is boiling in the cast iron) and do not like. You might want to cover the inside of the Dutch Oven with foil before cooking. Put hot charcoals on the top of the Dutch Oven lid and 5-6 on the bottom. You will probably want 70% of the lid covered in hot charcoals. I suggest using your smaller Dutch Ovens for this (not the super teeny tiny ones though).

Suggested Fire:

- o Charcoal Fire

Tools Required:

- o Cast iron Dutch Oven

Ingredients:

- o Bacon (not required though suggested)
- o Can(s) of beans
- o Brown sugar (not required though suggested)

Service Size: Listed on the can of beans

Baked Potatoes

Baked potatoes are one of the easiest dishes to prepare, virtually requiring no food preparation. Completes just about any meal. Put the potatoes in the Dutch Oven and cook. Very simple. You do not need to wrap them in foil because the Dutch Oven acts as the foil.

Suggested Fire:

- o Charcoal fire

Tools Required:

- o Dutch oven
- o Kitchen tongs and/or heavy duty gloves

Ingredients:

- o Potatoes
- o Water

Serving Size: 1 person per potato

Preparation:

1. Place potatoes in Dutch oven. Can layer potatoes up to two deep
2. Place 1 cup water into the Dutch oven
3. Cover with Dutch oven lid
4. Place coals for fire on top of Dutch oven and place Dutch oven on top of a few coals
5. Allow to cook for 1 hour

Bar-B-Que Loin

One of the best camping foods you will ever eat. Fill up the Dutch Oven, as shown, with BBQ sauce. Be prepared to put in up to 1 gallon of sauce. Put in the cut up loins. Estimate a quarter pound (4 oz) per person. Let it sit until cooked. This will probably cook for 3-4 hours. Take out and serve when the meat is 140 degrees Fahrenheit.

My mouth is watering looking at this picture

Christmas comes early when you're cooking (after having read this book)

Breakfast Sausage, Fried

Place breakfast sausage in cast iron skillet, and cover with water. It is best to use a skillet with a cover. Cook until no read color on interior of the sausage. Remove water when sausage is cooked and further cook for a minute or two to remove excess water on the sausage.

Suggested Fire:

- o   Gas camp stove fire

Tools Required:

- o   Cast iron frying pan
- o   Spatula

Ingredients:

- o   Sausage links
- o   Water

Service Size: 4 people per ½ lb of sausage

Corn on the Cobb – Boiled

Corn on the cob is a standard outdoor dinner item that all too often gets left out of menu. This side dish is easy to prepare and almost cannot be ruined. Very common during the summer. Place dehusked corn in pot of required size. Sprinkle salt into water and add some oil (or even better yet some butter). Cover pot and bring to a boil. Corn is done when you can "pop" a kernel with your finger-nail. Usually it takes 10 minutes in boiling water to cook.

Suggested Fire:

- Gas camp stove fire or even wood/charcoal fire

Tools Required:

- Stainless steel or aluminum stock pot
- Kitchen tongs

Ingredients:

- o Corn on the cob
- o Water
- o Salt
- o Butter

Service Size: 1 ear per person

Corn on the Cobb – Baked

Corn on the cob is a standard outdoor dinner item that all too often gets left out of menu. This side dish is easy to prepare and almost cannot be ruined. If it's a tiny bit burnt, that's okay because "you can't see it from the highway".

Suggested Fire:

- o Charcoal fire

Tools Required:

- o Dutch oven
- o Kitchen tongs and/or heat resistant gloves

Ingredients:

- o Corn on the cob
- o Water
- o Salt
- o Butter

Service Size: 1 ear per person

French Toast

French toast is an easy and tasty variation on eggs for breakfast. It is pancakes meets scrambled eggs. You get the best of both aspects.

Suggested Fire:

- o Gas camp stove fire

Tools Required:

- o Cast Iron skillet or fry pan

Ingredients:

- o 3 eggs
- o ¼ cup milk
- o ½ teaspoon vanilla
- o ½ teaspoon ground cinnamon
- o 10 slices of bread
- o Maple syrup (optional)

Serving Size: 4

Preparation:

1. Crack eggs into a bowl
2. Add milk, cinnamon and vanilla
3. Using whisk, mix ingredients
4. Cut bread into diagonal halves
5. Set gas fire to medium heat/flame
6. Dip slice of bread into egg mixture and then place on skillet
7. Let cook for about 1 minute

8. Pour maple syrup over the toast when served

Grilled Cheese Sandwiches

Serves/Makes: 1

Ingredients:
2 slices of bread (preferably Texas Toast)

1 or 2 slices of cheese singles

Butter

Tools:
Spatula

Skillet

Camp stove

Directions:

Add butter to 1 side of each piece of bread. Put the butter-side down piece of bread on one. Put the cheese on top of it. Put the bread butter-side up on top of it. Grill on skillet and flip with spatula until golden brown or cheese is melted.

Grilled Steaks

Ready in: < 30 minutes

Serves/Makes: 4

2 tablespoons commercial steak seasoning

4 (6 oz. ea.) beef tenderloin steaks

1 tablespoon vegetable oil

Directions:

Preheat grill to medium-high heat. Place commercial steak seasoning in ziplock bag. Place steak in bag and "toss" till steak is covered with seasoning.

Grill 6 to 8 minutes on each side or until cooked to desired doneness.

Pop Corn

This is a simple, easy to prepare item that can liven up any campout. The vast majority of people have never even thought of this simple treat while camping.

Suggested Fire:

- o Gas camp stove fire

Tools Required:

- o Large stainless steel or aluminum stock pot with lid

Ingredients:

- o Popping corn

- o Vegetable oil. You can also use flavored popcorn popping oil
- o Salt, fine ground

Serving Size: 10

Preparation:

1. Cover the bottom of the stock pot with a single layer of popping corn
2. Cover the layer of popping corn with vegetable oil
3. Place the cover on the stock pot and place on the gas fire.
4. Move/slide the pot around on top of the fire. Do not stop movement of the pot
5. Once the popping starts, keep moving the pot on the fire until you hear the popping start to slow down.
6. Remove the pot from the fire.
7. Add salt to taste. Can also use butter flavors popcorn salt if desired

Scrambled Eggs

Ingredients:

- 4 lg. eggs
- 1/4 c. milk
- 1/2 tsp. salt
- 1/2 tsp. pepper
- 2 tbsp. butter
- 1 oz. vegetable oil

Suggested fire:

- camp stove

Tools required:

- Spatula
- Skillet

Mix the milk, eggs, salt and pepper, and butter in a mixing bowl. Pour into your skillet. Have temperature be between low and medium. Stir with spatula until they are as scrambled as you want them to be. You get great taste from the cast iron.

.

Basic Recipes

Beef Stew

Ingredients (per 4 people)
1 pound beef stew meat (cut into cubes about 1 each in size)
2 to 3 potatoes. Peeled and then cut into pieces
Bag of peeled baby carrots
1 onion (peeled and cut up)
1 can tomato soup.

In cast iron skillet, brown the stew meat with salt, pepper and the onion.
Drain and transfer the meat/onion mixture to a stock pot.
Added potatoes, carrots and tomato soup to the pot. Add water till
mixture is covered. Simmer till meat is cooked.

Beef Stroganoff

Ingredients (per 4 people)
1 pound cubed (cut into cubes about 1 inch in size) stew meat
1 onion chopped
1 can mushroom soup
Small can of mushrooms (can be stems and pieces or cut up whole
mushrooms)
1 cup sour cream (can substitute with yogurt)
Salt/pepper
Noodles (egg noodles)

In cast iron skillet, brown stew meat along with salt and pepper and cut
up onion. When the meat is brown, stir in can of mushroom soup and
simmer till meat is cooked, then add sour cream. In a separate pot boil
water and prepare the noodles. Drain water from noodles.
Put noodles on each person's plate and cover with meat mixture.

Camp Oven Biscuits

These are very simple. You just buy pre-canned biscuits from the grocery store in one of those cylinders. You open them, space them out, and cook until golden brown. The camp oven literally acts like your oven at home. Doing this on a camp oven can also free up a Dutch Oven for an entrée.

Ingredients:
Pre-canned biscuits

Tools:
Camp Oven
Stove

Chicken Noodle Soup

This is a classic campout meal. Great for lunch and dinner. You can either just buy cans of it from the store, stick them all in the stainless steel pot, and boil. You can also make it yourself. Just buy some chicken, celery, carrots, onions, and get some water. Cut up everything, fry the chicken a bit on a skillet, dump everything in the pot, add water, and boil that. Very tasty.

Tasty and healthy

Chicken Quesadillas

Suggested Fire:

- o Gas camp stove fire

Tools Required:

- o Cast iron fry pan or skillet
- o Spatula

Ingredients:

- o 12 oz cooked chicken breasts, diced
- o 2/3 cup shredded cheese. Monterey jack cheese or a "Mexican" mix works best
- o 8 (8") flour tortillas

- o Salsa
- o Sour cream
- o Vegetable oil

Serving Size: 4

Preparation:

1. Set gas stove to medium flame/heat
2. Dice chicken breast meat. If cold, heat in a pot

3. Place flour tortilla on oiled fry pan surface

4. Sprinkle cheese onto tortilla

5. Sprinkle diced chicken breast meat on top of cheese

6. Sprinkle cheese on top of breast meat

7. Place flour tortilla on top of cheese/chicken mixture

8. Flip "tortilla sandwich" oven when bottom tortilla is browned (approximately 1 minute)

9. Remove from skillet after another minute or so

Dutch Oven Biscuits

Ready in: < 30 minutes

Ingredients:
Pre-made biscuits that come in those cylinder cans from the store

Tools:
Dutch Oven
Gloves
Tongs
Foil (suggested but not necessary)

Suggested fire:
Charcoal fire

Like most recipes in this book, we do not suggest making things from scratch. We highly suggest using biscuits pre-made from the grocery store. Cover the Dutch Oven's insides in foil (not required though suggested). Put in the biscuits spaced out how the directions specify on the can – usually an inch. Place coals on the top covering 50-75% and 5-7 on the bottom. Cook until golden brown on the top (usually after 10-20 minutes, you need to check every couple minutes). Then, using the tongs, flip them to the other side. Cook the other side to be golden brown (again 10-20 minutes). Then take them out with the tongs. These are very simple and tasty.

Flipping the biscuits is an art

Lasagna

Ingredients (per 6 people)
1 pound of ground beef
¼ pound of lasagna noodles (approximately 8 lasagna noodles)
1 28 oz jar of spaghetti sauce
2/3 pound of cottage cheese
¼ pound of Parmesan cheese
¼ pound of Mozzarella cheese

Brown ground beef with some salt and pepper. Boil water in a stock pot with salt and oil added, and prepare the lasagna noodles as indicated (usually this means placing the noodle sin the boiling water for 7 minutes). Drain water from the noodles using a colander. Allow noodles to cool (they would burn your hands if you tray and handle them right after they have been cooked in boiling water). Using the cooled noodles, fill the Dutch oven by layering the noodles with the meat, cheese and spaghetti sauce. If you are doing anything special like cooking Italian sausages, place them on the top of the lasagna. Place coals on the top of the Dutch oven and a few below. Cook till the lasagna starts to bubble.

Shepherd's Pie

Ingredients (per 6 people):
1 pound ground beef
1 onion
1 can of cream of mushroom soup
1 can of mixed vegetables (or if you are feeding a younger crowd, ½ can of corn and 1/2 can of peas)
Instant mashed potatoes
Shredded cheese

Brown ground beef with some salt and pepper along with the onion (of course the onion needs to have been peeled and cut up into slices beforehand) added in cast iron skillet.   When brown, stir in canned vegetables and cream of mushroom soup. Transfer the mixture to a Dutch oven. Make enough mashed potatoes to cover the mixture in the Dutch oven and sprinkle shredded cheese over the top of the mashed potatoes.   Place coals on top of the Dutch oven, and a coal or two under the Dutch over. Cook till the mixture starts to bubble.

Turkey Breast

You can do 2 at a time, but don't be surprised if only 1 fits

Ready in: 2.5+ hrs

Serves/Makes: 14

Ingredients:
Turkey breast(s)
Salt and pepper
Other seasonings of your choosing

Tools Required:
Dutch Oven
Gloves
Meat thermometer

Suggested Fire:
Charcoal fire

Directions:

Put turkey in the Dutch Oven. There doesn't need to be any liquid at the bottom or anything like that that doesn't come from the turkey itself. Maybe a little water, but that is not necessary. Pour salt and pepper (and your seasoning if you want) on the turkey. Get that bird covered for the most part. Then put on the lid of the Dutch Oven. Put coals on the top of the Dutch oven that cover 80% of it. You can add more later if they are needed. Also put 6-7 coals on the bottom of the Dutch Oven too. Now you just sit and wait until the Turkey is finished. Stop cooking when the internal temperature is 185-190 degrees Fahrenheit.

Desserts

What campout would be complete without some mouth watering desserts? One of our favorite statements, is "that just because its camping doesn't mean you have to be miserable", and a corollary to this is that "just because you are camping doesn't mean you have to eat bland/boring food".

A favorite tradition of Boy Scout gatherings is a thing called the "cracker barrel". In theory, this 'informal gathering" is a wide selection of finger foods from each troop trying to show off their cooking abilities. In reality, it is mainly each troop preparing a dessert that they share (since these things normally don't start till after 9:00 PM), and in some cases it does showcase a troop's culinary skills.

As already described, the Dutch oven is the perfect tool to prepare a wide variety of desserts, but we have found to really make a campout a remembered event, desserts all day long are required, much like in days of old when we went to visit grandmother and she baked pies and cookies the whole time you were there. So not all of our recipes require or utilize a Dutch oven, and in the case of cookies we utilize the camp store almost exclusively.

Brownies

What you need: Brownie mix (and ingredients that your brownie mix requires)
Suggested fire type: Charcoal fire
Tools: Dutch Oven (on the smaller side is preferred)

Making brownies in a Dutch Oven is just like at home. You make the brownie mix (you can make from scratch but just realize that this is messier and takes more time). Put it in the Dutch Oven and cook for 20-40 minutes with 6-8 coals on top and 3-5 on the bottom. Check to see if it is still uncooked by sticking a knife in it and pulling it out every 5-6 minutes after 15 minutes of cooking. If there is stuff on the knife, then you know it is still cooking. They need to cool before serving.

Dump Cake/Cobbler

2 cans of fruit pie filling

1 package white cake mix (can use 2 also though we suggest 1)

1 stick of butter

Pour pie filling in seasoned Dutch Oven (10 in. Dutch Oven using this recipe should feed 7-8). Mix cake mix into batter per instructions on the box.

There are various styles:

1 – Mix the filling with the cake mix/batter (generally pouring the mix straight out of the box onto the pie filling and mixing it will make the batter) to have a consistent mix throughout the Dutch Oven. Also mix in a stick of butter

2 – Pour on the pie filling first, then cake mix/batter second and just let it sit there... stir the cake mix/batter around the top that way there isn't a pyramid of cake mix/batter. Throw a stick of butter on the top

3 – Pour the cake mix in first, stir it all around the bottom of the Dutch Oven, and then pour the pie filling on. Throw on the stick of butter too on the top. We do not suggest doing this because of high likelihood of food getting burnt,

4 – Put in a stick of butter on the bottom, let it melt, and spread it around the bottom. Pour on the pie filling. Pour on the batter. Have the batter be across the top. Do NOT stir.

Put 4-6 coals on bottom and then put hot coals on top of the lid (8 - 10). Cook for 25 - 35 minutes. Check occasionally so that spots don't burn.

Peanut Butter Cookies

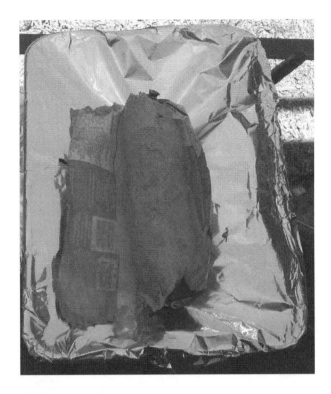

Ready in: < 30 minutes

Peanut Butter cookies, although not as popular as sugar cookies, are just as easy to make and satisfy many stomachs. Very simple directions are to buy the pre-made dough (or make it yourself… recipes found online) and make 4-5 balls to put on the metal plate. Cook until lightly golden brown and cool. Seriously, you will be amazed at them

Bake for 8 - 10 minutes at 325 degrees

You can never have enough

Sugar Cookies

Between meals, there is nothing that tames the wild beast at a campout than sugar cookies. Cooking cookies also clearly shows mastery of the outdoor kitchen. Basic directions are to buy the pre-made dough (or make it yourself… recipes found online) and make 4-5 balls to put on the metal plate. Cook until lightly golden brown and cool. Seriously, you will be amazed at them. Oatmeal cookies follow the same instructions.

Suggested Fire:

- o Gas camp stove fire

Tools Required:

- o Box oven

o Small metal plate
o Heat resistant gloves

Ingredients:

o Store purchased cookie dough

Or

o Sugar
o Flour
o Eggs

Camp Cook Checklist

Kevin serving scrambled eggs on a troop campout

Dutch Ovens & Related Tools

_____ Gloves, short

_____ Gloves, gauntlet

_____ Lid lifter

_____ Dutch Oven Table

_____ 8 inch Dutch Oven

_____ 10 inch Dutch Oven

_____ 10 inch Dutch Oven

_____ 12 inch Dutch Oven

_____ 12 inch Deep Dutch Oven

_____ Cast Iron Frying Pan

_____ Oil pan, glass jar or oil bucket

_____ Ash pan or bucket

_____ Ash/Coals shovel

Fire Making Tools

_____ Charcoal chimney

_____ Newspaper (for starting charcoal)

_____ Two 20 pound bags of charcoal

_____ Strike anywhere matches

_____ Two water buckets for putting a fire out

Sanitation & Cleanup Tools

_____ Big trash bags

_____ Trash Can or Bucket Ring & rope to hang from overhead

_____ Paper towels

_____ Hand sanitizer

Safety

_____ First Aid Kit

_____ large cotton towel

_____ Measuring spoons

_____ Plastic measuring cups

_____ bread knife

_____ wooden cutting Boards

_____ two hand towels

_____ can opener

____ olive oil in can

_____ plastic silverware

_____ paper plates

_____ coffee pot

_____ coffee cups

_____ paper plates

_____ one serving spoon per dish

_____ wooden spoons for stirring

_____ wooden spatula

_____ aluminum foil

_____ plastic wrap

_____ ziplock bags

_____ Tupperware bowls

_____ meat turner

_____ igloo for ingredients

_____ soft plastic scrubber

_____ liquid soap

_____ kitchen knives

Drinks & Drink Makings

_____ bottled water

_____ coffee (instant, tea bag style)

_____ ice tea mix

_____ instant hot coca mix

Condiments (taken regardless of menu)

_____ Ketchup

_____ mustard

_____ soy sauce

_____ sweet and low

_____ coffee creamer

_____ salt/pepper shakers

Basic Food (as dictated by menus planned)

_____ bacon

_____ cinnamon

_____ corn meal

_____ corn starch

_____ black pepper

_____ baking soda

_____ baking powder

_____ bouillon cubes

_____ butter

_____ carrots

_____ cheese

_____ coffee, ground

_____ creamer for coffee

_____ eggs

_____ flour

_____ garlic

_____ hot chocolate mix

_____ ice

_____ molasses

_____ olive oil

_____ onions

_____ pecans

_____ pepper

_____ Biscuit & Baking Mix

_____ potatoes

_____ rice

_____ salt

_____ sugar, white

_____ sugar, brown

_____ vanilla

_____ vinegar

_____ flour

_____ yeast

Common Abbreviations

Abbreviation	Meaning		Abbreviation	Meaning
bch	Bunch		oz	Ounce
bu	Bushel		pt	Pint
c	Cup		qt	Quart
doz	Dozen		Tbsp	Tablespoon
fl oz	Fluid Ounce		tsp	Teaspoon
g	Gram		pkg	Package
gal	Gallon		Serv	Serving
l	Liter		wt	Weight
lb	Pound			
ml	Milliliter			

Units of Measurement

Liquid Measures						
tsp	Tbsp	fl oz	c	pt	qt	gal
1/4	1/12	1/24				
1/2	1/6	1/12				
3/4	1/4	1/8				
1	1/3	1/6				
1 1/2	1/2	1/4				
2	2/3	1/3				
2 1/2	5/6	2/5				
3	1	1/2	1/16			
4	1 1/3	2/3	1/12			
5	1 2/3	5/6	1/9			
6	2	1	1/8			
12	4	2	1/4	1/8	3/50	1/64
18	6	3	3/8	1/6	1/11	1/43
24	8	4	1/2	1/4	1/8	1/32
36	12	6	3/4	1/3	1/6	3/64
48	16	8	1	1/2	1/4	1/16
96	32	16	2	1	1/2	1/8
120	40	20	2 1/2	1 1/5	3/5	1/6
144	48	24	3	1 4/9	5/7	1/5
192	64	32	4	2	1	1/4
384	128	64	8	4	2	1/2
492	164	82	10	5	2 1/2	2/3
576	192	96	12	6	3	3/4
768	256	128	16	8	4	1

Dry Measures

tsp	Tbsp	oz	c	lb	pt	qt	gal	pk	bu
1/4	1/12								
1/2	1/6								
3/4	1/4								
1	1/3								
1 1/2	1/2								
2	2/3								
2 1/2	5/6								
3	1	1/2	1/16						
4	1 1/3	2/3	1/12						
5	1 2/3	5/6	1/9						
6	2	1	1/8	1/16	1/16				
12	4	2	1/4	1/8	1/8	1/16			
18	6	3	3/8	1/5	1/5	1/10			
24	8	4	1/2	1/4	1/4	1/8			
36	12	6	3/4	3/8	3/8	3/16			
48	16	8	1	1/2	1/2	1/4	1/16	1/32	
96	32	16	2	1	1	1/2	1/8	1/16	
120	40	20	2 1/2	1 1/4	1 1/4	5/8	5/16	5/32	
144	48	24	3	1 1/2	1 1/2	3/4	3/16	3/32	
192	64	32	4	2	2	1	1/4	1/8	1/32
384	128	64	8	4	4	2	1/2	1/4	1/16
492	164	82	10	5	5 1/8	2 9/16			
576	192	96	12	6	6	3	3/4	3/8	3/32
768	256	128	16	8	8	4	1	1/2	1/8

How Much Meat to Buy[7]

The amount of meat to purchase is usually a function of delivering a 3oz serving to the plate. With that said, remember three important items: 1) that's a cooked 3 oz serving, and 2) not all meat cooks up the same, and 3) skin on/off and bone in/out makes a difference on the usable amount of meat per pound. The table below gives an approximate number of servings per pound of meat.

Beef	Approximate number of servings per pound (16 oz)
Brisket	4
Ground Beef (lean)	4
Stew Meat	3
Porterhouse Steak	4
T-Bone Steak	4
Rump roast (bone-in)	3
Rump Roast (Boneless)	5

---

[7] USDA home and garden Bulletin #265

Chicken	Approximate number of servings per pound (16 oz)
Bone-in with skin	3
Boneless and skinless	5
Chicken Wings	1.5
Drumsticks	2.5
Thighs	4

Pork	Approximate number of servings per pound (16 oz)
Boneless Chops	5
Center-cut loin chops	5
Ham bone-in	4
Spareribs	2
Tenderloin	5

Herbs & Spices

Herbs[8]

Herbs	Source	Description	Flavor	Traditional/Typical Application[9]
Basil	California, Hungary, France, Yugoslavia	Leaves. Usually marked as small bits of green leaves. **Available:** whole and ground.	Aromatic, faintly anise like, mildly pungent taste.	**Flavor uses:** Pizza and spaghetti sauces, stewed tomatoes, vegetable soup, salad dressings, poultry stuffings. **Garnish uses:** stuffings, tomato sauces.
Bay Leaves	Turkey, Portugal	Elliptical leaves, up to 3 in. long, deep green pper surface, paler underneath. **Available:** whole or ground.	Fragrant, sweetly aromatic, sightly bitter taste.	**Flavor uses:** Beef stew, chicken pie, salami, dill and sour pickles, stewed tomatoes, oxtail and pepper pot soups. **Garnish uses:** Pickled meats, salad dressings.

---

[8] American Spice Trade Association
[9] In most situations, foods are seasoned with a combination of spices. The typical/traditional uses for each listed spice simply indicates inclusion in that food item and not as the only spice used.

Herbs	Source	Description	Flavor	Traditional/Typical Application[9]
Dill Seed	India	Light brown, oval seeds, 3/32-3/16-in. long. **Available:** whole and ground.	Clean, aromatic odor, warm, caraway-like taste	**Flavor uses:** Dill pickles, French dressing, pickled beans and beets, cheese dips, fish sauces. **Garnish uses:** Pickles, spiced vegetables, marinated shrimp.
Fennel Seed	India, Argentina	Green to yellowish brown seeds, oblong oval, 5/32-5/16-in. long. **Available:** whole and ground.	Warm, sweet, anise-like odor and taste.	**Flavor uses:** Italian sausage, Italian bread, oxtail soup, Pizza and spaghetti sauces, sweet pickles, fish sauces. **Garnish uses:** Italian breads and baked goods.

Herbs	Source	Description	Flavor	Traditional/Typical Application[9]
Marjoram	France, Portugal, Greece, Rumania	As marketed, small pieces of grayish-green leaves. **Available:** whole and ground.	Warm, aromatic, pleasantly bitter, slightly camphoraceous.	**Flavor uses:** Chicken casseroles, ham and liver spreads, goulash, Polish, liver and summer sausages, herb dressing, stuffing's, ravioli, herbed breads. **Garnish uses:** Salad dressings, stuffing's, herbed breads.
Oregano	Greece, Mexico, Japan	As marketed, small pieces of green leaves. **Available:** whole and ground.	Strong, pleasant, somewhat camphoraceous odor and taste.	**Flavor uses:** Chili con carne, pizza and spaghetti sauces, lasagna, tamales, enchiladas, cocktail dips snacks, sloppy Joes, Italian green beans. **Garnish uses:** Pizza, Italian sauces, salad dressings.

Herbs	Source	Description	Flavor	Traditional/Typical Application[9]
Parsley Flakes	California, Texas	Flakes of bright green leaves. Also granulated.	Characteristic, mild, agreeable odor and taste.	**Flavor uses:** Chicken soup, chicken pot pie, fish sauces, cocktail dips, French and herb dressings. **Garnish uses:** Salad dressings, stuffing's, soups, sauced vegetable combinations, cottage cheese.
Rosemary	France, Spain, Portugal, California	Bits of pine needle-like green leaves. **Available:** whole and ground.	Agreeable aromatic odor, fresh, bittersweet taste.	**Flavor uses:** Herb dressing, stuffing's, chicken stew, herbed bread, carrots, Potatoes. **Garnish uses:** Salad dressings, herb bread.
Sage	Yugoslavia, Albania	Oblate-lanceolate shaped leaves, grayish green, about 3-in. long. **Available:** whole, cut, rubbed, ground.	Highly aromatic, with strong, warm, slightly bitter taste.	**Flavor uses:** Pork sausage, pizza sauce, chicken pot pie, meat loaf, sauerbraten, stuffing's, cheese, veal loaf. **Garnish uses:** Pork sausage, poultry stuffing, seasoned bread crumbs.

Herbs	Source	Description	Flavor	Traditional/Typical Application[9]
Savory	France, Spain	As marketed, bits of dried greenish-brown leaves. **Available:** whole and ground.	Fragrant, aromatic odor.	**Flavor uses:** Chicken pot pie, Salami, herb bread, herbed dressing, herbed rice, stuffing's, creamed onions. **Garnish uses:** herb dressing, stuffing's, herb bread.
Tarragon	California, France, Yugoslavia	As marketed, bits of green leaves. **Available:** whole and ground.	Sweet, aromatic, anise-like odor and taste.	**Flavor uses:** Herb salad dressing, cocktail dips, stuffing's, casseroles, vinegars. **Garnish uses:** Salad dressings, herb vinegars, sauces.
Thyme	Spain, France	As marketed, bits of grayish to greenish-brown leaves. **Available:** whole and ground.	Fragrant, aromatic odor, warm, quite pungent taste	**Flavor uses:** Sauerbraten, chicken pie, pizza and other Italian-style sauces, clam chowder, consommé, mock turtle and vegetable soups, herb dressings and vinegars, stuffing's, salami and liver sausages. **Garnish uses:** Salad dressings, clam chowder, oyster stew, herb vinegar.

Spices[10]

Spice	Source	Description	Flavor	Traditional/Typical Application[11]
Allspice	Jamaica, Honduras, Mexico	Reddish-brown berries. 1/8 – 5/16 in. diameter. **Available:** whole and ground.	Pungent, clove-like odor and taste.	**Favor uses:** baked beans, frankfurters, Polish sausage, sweet pickles & relishes, chili sauce, tomato and vegetable soups, cookies, pastries. **Garnish uses:** pickles, relishes.
Anise Seed	Spain, Netherlands, Mexico	Greenish-brown, ovoid-shaped seeds, 3/16 in. long. **Available:** whole and ground.	Pleasant, licorice like odor and taste.	**Flavor uses**: cookies, sweet rolls, fruit fillings, candies.

---

[10] American Spice Trade Association

[11] In most situations, foods are seasoned with a combination of spices. The typical/traditional uses for each listed spice simply indicates inclusion in that food item and not as the only spice used.

Spice	Source	Description	Flavor	Traditional/Typical Application[11]
Caraway Seeds	Netherlands, Poland	Curved, tapered brown seeds, up to 1/4-in. long. **Available:** whole.	Characteristic odor, warm, slightly sharp taste.	**Flavor uses:** Rye bread, crackers, cheese, cocktail dips, sauerkraut, sweet pickles. **Garnish uses:** Rye bread, salt sticks, crackers, cheese, coleslaw, sauerkraut
Cardamon Seeds	Guatemala, India	Small, angular reddish-brown seeds, often marketed in their pods— greenish or buff colored (blanched). **Available:** whole, decorticated and ground.	Pleasantly fragrant odor, slightly sharp taste.	**Flavor uses:** Coffee cake, sweet pickles, French salad dressing, marmalade, frankfurters. **Garnish uses:** Coffee (Middle Eastern-style).

114

Spice	Source	Description	Flavor	Traditional/Typical Application[11]
Celery Flakes	California	Medium to dark green flakes, about 3/8-in. diameter. **Available:** flakes, granulated and powdered.	Sweet, strong typical celery odor and taste.	**Flavor uses:** Dry soups, casserole mixes, stuffings, soups, stewed tomatoes. **Garnish uses:** Potato salads, meat sauces.
Celery Seed	India, France	Grayish-brown seed, up to 1/16-in. diameter. **Available:** whole, ground and salt	Warm, slightly bitter celery odor and taste	**Flavor uses:** Beef stew, meat loaf, dill, sweet and mixed vegetable pickles, barbecue, chili and ketchup sauces, chicken, clam, oyster, and vegetable soups, French dressing. **Garnish uses:** Cole slaw, salad dressings, pickles.

Spice	Source	Description	Flavor	Traditional/Typical Application[11]
Chili Powder	California	Red to very dark red powder.	Characteristic, aromatic odor with varying levels of heat or pungency.	**Flavor uses:** Chili con carne, tacos, sweet, sour and mixed vegetable pickles, tamale pie, Swiss steak, sloppy Joes, barbecue sauce, potato chips and crackers, cocktail dips, tomato ketchup, salad dressing, miscellaneous snack foods. **Garnish uses:** potato chips, crackers, cheese, chili, baked fish.
Chives (freeze dried)	California	Bright green, cross-cut sections of the tubular shoots, about 1/8-in.	Mild, delicate onion odor and taste.	**Flavor uses:** Cottage cheese, soup mixes, cocktail dips, casseroles, sour cream dressings, omelets. **Garnish uses:** Cottage cheese, sour cream, salad

Spice	Source	Description	Flavor	Traditional/Typical Application[11]
Cinnamon	Indonesia, Seychelles, Ceylon, Taiwan	Tan to reddish brown quills(sticks) of rolled bark, varying lengths. Available: whole and ground.	Agreeable aromatic with sweet, pungent taste.	**Flavor uses:** Sweet and apple based baked goods, apple sauce and butter, baked beans, sweet and mixed vegetable pickles, chili sauce, pickled beets, prune butter, spiced fruits, ketchup. **Garnish uses:** Pickles, relishes, pickled meats and seafood, spiced fruit.
Cloves	Malagasy Republic, Indonesia, Tanzania	Reddish-brown, 1/2-3/4-in. long. Available: whole and ground.	Strong, pungent, sweet odor and taste.	**Flavor uses:** Backed beans, potted chicken, dill, sweet and mixed vegetable pickles, barbecue sauce, pickled beets, prune butter, spiced fruits, ketchup, steak sauce, okra and tomato soup, cakes, French dressing, deviled chicken, frankfurters, liver sausage and spreads, cookies, fruit pastries, candies, backed ham. **Garnish uses:** Pickles, relishes, ham, cookies.

Spice	Source	Description	Flavor	Traditional/Typical Application[11]
Coriander Seed	Morocco, Rumania, Lebanon	Yellowish-brown, nearly globular seed, 1/2-3/16-in. diameter **Available:** whole and ground.	Distinctively fragrant, lemon-like odor and taste.	**Flavor uses:** Frankfurters, ham spread, bologna sausage, bean, oxtail and okra soups, dill and mixed vegetable pickles, salami, steak sauce. **Garnish uses:** Pickles.
Cumin Seed	Iran, India, Lebanon	Yellowish-brown, elongated oval seeds, 1/8-1/4-in. diameter. **Available:** whole and ground.	Strong aromatic, somewhat bitter.	**Flavor uses:** Chili con carne, barbecue sauce, taco sauce, tamale pie, enchiladas, Spanish rice, cheese spreads.

Spice	Source	Description	Flavor	Traditional/Typical Application[11]
Fenugreek Seed	India, France, Lebanon, Argentina	Small, flat, squares-shaped seeds, yellowish-brown, each with a deep furrow. **Available:** whole and ground.	Strong, sweet odor with burnt sugar-like taste.	**Flavor uses:** Curry powder, imitation maple flavor, Chutney, pickles.
Garlic (dried)	California	White material, ranging in standard particle size from: powdered, granulated, ground, minced, chopped, large chopped: sliced, large sliced.	Strong, characteristic odor, extremely pungent taste.	**Flavor uses:** Chicken pot pie, all Italian and Mexican specialties, Spanish rice, macaroni and cheese, Salami, Polish and Italian sausages, barbecue steak, ketchup sauces, salad dressings, cocktail dips, snack foods, bread, bean soup, pot roast and stews. **Garnish uses:** Salad dressings, Italian bread, pickles vegetables.

Spice	Source	Description	Flavor	Traditional/Typical Application[11]
Ginger	Nigeria, Sierra Leone, Jamaica	Irregularly shaped pieces("hands") 2 1/2-4 in. long, brownish to buff colored (when peeled and bleached). **Available:** whole, ground, cracked.	Pungent, spicy-sweet odor, clean, hot taste.	**Flavor uses:** Chinese foods, cookies, cakes, macaroni and cheese, summer sausage, sweet and dill pickles, chili sauce, marmalade, French dressing, frankfurters and bologna, chicken soup, glazed carrots. **Garnish uses:** Pickles, relishes, pickled meats.
Mace	Indonesia, Granada	Flat, brittle pieces of lacy material, yellow to brownish-orange in color. **Available:** whole and ground.	See nutmeg, but somewhat stronger, less delicate.	**Flavor uses:** Baked beans, ketchup and steak sauce, clam, oyster, split pea and chicken soups, French dressing, frankfurters, bologna, chicken, ham and liver spreads, cakes, cookies, fruit pies and pastries.

Spice	Source	Description	Flavor	Traditional/Typical Application[11]
Mustard	Canada, Denmark, United Kingdom, United States	Tiny, smooth, nearly globular seeds, yellowish or reddish-brown. **Available:** whole and ground.	**Yellow:** no odor, but sharp, pungent taste when water is added. **Brown:** with water added, sharp, irritating odor, pungent taste.	**Flavor uses:** Macaroni and cheese, sweet, dill, mixed vegetable and bread and butter pickles, barbecue sauce, chutney, chow sauce and ketchup, French dressing, mayonnaise, deviled ham, bologna, frankfurter, salami and summer sausages, cocktail dips, cheese spreads. **Garnish uses:** Pickles, relishes, pickled meats, salad dressings.
Nutmeg	Indonesia, Granada	Large brown, ovular seed, up to 1 1/4-in. long. **Available:** whole and ground.	Characteristic, sweet, warm odor and taste.	**Flavor uses:** Cakes, cookies, pastries, eggnog, puddings, salami, frankfurters, Polish and smoked sausages, chow sauce, spinach soup, ravioli, spiced fruit. **Garnish uses:** Eggnog, custards, puddings.

Spice	Source	Description	Flavor	Traditional/Typical Application[11]
Onion (dried)	California	White material ranging in particle size from: powdered, granulated, ground, minced, chopped, large chopped, sliced, large sliced.	Sweetly pungent onion odor and taste.	**Flavor uses:** Ketchup, soups, meats, pickles, sauces, dressings, Chinese foods, Spanish rice, vegetables, chili con carne, omelets. **Garnish uses:** Relishes, salad dressings.
Paprika	California, Spain, Bulgaria, Morocco, South Africa	Powder, ranging in color from bright, rich red to brick-red, depending on the variety and handling.	Slightly sweet odor and taste may have moderate bite.	**Flavor uses:** Chorizo, frankfurter, bologna and Italian sausages, barbecue sauce, ketchup, French dressing, mayonnaise, cheese, cocktail dips, snacks, stew, goulash, chili con carne. **Garnish uses:** Salad dressing, sausages, casserole-type dishes, cottage cheese, soups, backed fish, cheese dips.

Spice	Source	Description	Flavor	Traditional/Typical Application[11]
Rosemary	France, Spain, Portugal, California	Bits of pine needle-like green leaves. **Available:** whole and ground.	Agreeable aromatic odor, fresh, bittersweet taste.	**Flavor uses:** Herb dressing, stuffing's, chicken stew, herbed bread, carrots, Potatoes. **Garnish uses:** Salad dressings, herb bread.
Saffron	Spain, Portugal	Orange and yellow strands, approximately 1/2-3/4-in. long **Available:** whole and ground.	Highly aromatic, odor, fresh, bittersweet taste.	**Flavor uses:** Spanish rice, arroz con pollo, saffron rice. **Garnish uses:** Rice, Spanish-type casseroles, bread.
Sesame Seed	Mexico, Nicaragua, Guatemala, Salvador, United States	Hulled seed, creamy or pearly white, flattened, about 1/8-in. diameter. **Available:** whole (unhulled and hulled).	Mildly nutty odor and taste.	**Flavor uses:** Rolls, crackers, snacks, candy. **Garnish uses:** Rolls, breads, crackers, snacks

Spice	Source	Description	Flavor	Traditional/Typical Application[11]
Shallots (freeze dried)	California	1/4 x 3/8-in. white pieces.	Mild, but more aromatic onion odor and taste.	**Flavor uses:** Dairy products, sauce mixes, soups, prepared dishes. **Garnish uses:** Salad dressings, relishes.
Sweet Pepper Flakes	California	1/4 x 1/4-in. flakes. Bright green and red. Also granulated and powered.	Mild, slightly sweet odor, somewhat bittersweet taste.	**Flavor uses:** Soup mixes, canned soups, Spanish rice, corn Creole, stewed tomatoes, chili sauce, and refrigerated salads. **Garnish uses:** Relishes, salads, stewed tomatoes, dressings

Spice	Source	Description	Flavor	Traditional/Typical Application[11]
Pepper, Black	Indonesia, Brazil, India, Malaysia	Brownish-black wrinkled berries, up to 1/8-in. diameter. **Available:** whole, ground, cracked and decorticated	Characteristic, penetrating odor, hot biting taste.	**Flavor uses:** Beef stew, Brunswick stew, chicken gravy, corned beef hash, goulash, all Italian specialties, Spanish rice, Polish, summer, bologna, frankfurter, pork and liver sausages, French dressing, spinach, pepper pot and vegetable soups, barbecue sauce, dips and snacks. **Garnish uses:** Pickles, relishes, spiced meats and vegetables, salad dressing.
Pepper, White	Indonesia, Brazil, Malaysia	Yellowish-gray seed, up to 3/32-in. diameter. **Available:** whole and ground.	Like black pepper, but less pungent.	**Flavor uses:** All creamed soups, mayonnaise, ham and liver spread, deviled ham, chicken and tongue.

Spice	Source	Description	Flavor	Traditional/Typical Application[11]
Poppy Seed	Rumania, Turkey, Netherlands, Poland	Tiny round seeds, slate blue in color. **Available:** whole.	Mild, nut like odor and taste.	**Flavor uses:** Rolls, breads, pastry fillings, crackers, snacks, noodles. **Garnish uses:** Rolls, bread, crackers, cheese, cakes, and noodle puddings.
Pepper, Red	Japan, Mexico, Turkey, United States	Elongated and oblate-shaped red pods of varying sizes, from 3/8-12-in. depending on variety. **Available:** whole and ground.	Characteristic odor with heat levels mild to intensely pungent.	**Flavor uses:** Backed beans, Brunswick stew, sweet and sour pickles pickled pigs foot, bologna, smoked pork, frankfurter and fresh pork sausages, liver and ham spreads, chutney, ketchup, steak sauce. **Garnish uses:** Pickles, pickled meats, salad dressing.
Turmeric	India, Jamaica	Fibrous roots, orange-yellow in color, 1-3-in. long. **Available:** ground.	Characteristic odor, reminiscent of pepper, slightly bitter taste.	**Flavor uses:** Spanish rice, curries, pickles, relishes, margarine, cheeses, mustard, mayonnaise. **Garnish uses:** Pickles, relishes, sauces, prepared mustard.

Other Sources of Information

An outdoor palace

Books:

Camper's Guide to Outdoor Cooking, by John G. Ragsdale. 1989. Gulf Publishing Company. Paperback. 170 pages.

Cast Iron Cooking, by A.D. Livingston. 1991. The Lyons Press. Paperback. 143 pages.

Cooking for Groups. United States Department of Agriculture. 2001. paperback. 37 pages.

Cooking Under Cover, by Linda & Fred Griffith. 1996. Rand, McNally. Hardback. 351 pages.

Cooking the Dutch Oven Way, by Woody Woodruff. 1989. ICS Books, Inc. Paperback. 166 pages.

Cooking Over Coals, by Mel Marshall. 1971. Winchester Press. Hardback. 314 pages.

Cowboys and Cookouts: A taste of the old west. 2003. Barron's Educational Series, Inc. Hardback. 127 pages.

The Laclede Gas Cook Book by Mary Louise Bohn. 1956. Laclede Gas Company. Paperback. 160 pages.

Lodge Presents Chef John Flose's Cast Iron Cooking, by John Flose. 1999. Lodge Manufacturing Company. Paperback. 103 pages.

The Official Tex-Mex Cookbook by T.L. Bush. 1997. Gulf Publishing Company. 73 pages.

The Outward Bound Backpackers Handbook, by Glenn Randall. 1999. MJF Books. Paperback. 222 pages.

Old-Fashioned Dutch Oven Cookbook, by Don Holm. 1996. Caxton Printers, Ltd. Paperback. 131 pages.

Roughing It Easy, by Dian Thomas. 1975. Warner Books. Paperback. 246 pages.

The Spicy Camp Cookbook, by M. Timothy O'Keefe. 1997. Menasha Ridge Press. Paperback. 135 pages.

Spirit of The West: Cooking from Ranch House and Range, by Beverly Cox and Martin Jacobs. 1996. Artisan. Hardback. 224 pages.

The Trailside Cookbook: A handbook for hungry campers and hikers by Don and Pam Philpott. 2005. Firefly Books Ltd. Paperback. 144 pages.

World Championship Dutch Oven Cookbook, by Kohler and Michaud. 1989. Paperback. 88 pages.

Web Sites:

Boy Scout Troop 680's Recipe Library:
www.bsatroop680.org/documents/Cooking

Centers for Disease Control and Prevention: www.cdc.gov/foodsafety

Food and Drug Administration: www.cfsan.fda.gov

Food Safety and Inspection Services: www.fsis.usda.gov

Government Food Safety information: www.foodsafety.gov

Lodge Manufacturing Company: www.lodgemfg.com

Partnership for Food Safety Education (Fight BAC!): www.fightbac.org

The Authors

Dr. Michael Stachiw:

Dr. Stachiw not only has intimate knowledge of outdoor cooking through its practical application, but obtained his Ph.D. in food science from Michigan State University with a specialty area of meats and sausages. Dr Stachiw will be the first to point out that all the "textbook learning in the world cannot compensate for practical experience over the open flame". His Dutch Oven cooking has often been said to be better than most housewives.

Michael Stachiw, Jr.

Michael is an Eagle Scout with hundreds of nights of camping and a Philmont trek under his belt. After seeing fellow Scouts eating raw bacon and other mystery meat concoctions, he figured there has to be a better way to cook. His favorite Dutch Oven memory is eating cobbler for the first time